Louise Etheridge was born in Bradford-on-Avon, which is not Bradford. She was educated in Kent and Scotland and studied at Edinburgh University where she learned things that make her good in a pub quiz. After a fifteen-year 'portfolio' career in which she enjoyed numbers, helped to build satellites and forced people to learn to read, she gave it all up for a life of freedom and penury as a writer, poet and lyricist. *Slightly Wrong* is her first collection of poems and won't be her last. So hard luck.

"When I am low only an Etheridge poem will get me up to go. She is absurdly brilliant."

Sandi Toksvig

by the same author

More Slightly Wrong
Happy Stories for Busy People

LOUISE ETHERIDGE

Slightly Wrong

Angry Hen Press

First published in 2014
by Angry Hen Press
Reprinted 2015

All rights reserved
© Louise Etheridge, 2014

The legal stuff
This book is sold subject to the condition that it shall not, by way of trade or otherwise, be lent, resold, hired out or otherwise circulated without the publisher's prior consent in any form of binding of cover other than that in which it is published and without a similar condition including this condition begin imposed on the subsequent purchaser.

Not really sure what that meant. You are welcome to lend this book to your mates.

Although every precaution has been taken in the preparation of this book, the publisher and author assume no responsibility for errors or omissions. Neither is any liability assumed for damages resulting from the use of the information contained herein.

Louise Etheridge is hereby identified as author of this work in accordance with Section 77 of the Copyright, Designs and Patents Act 1988. So there.

No animals were harmed in the making of this book. Except kittens.

Not suitable for children

ISBN 978-0-9574315-8-4

www.louiseetheridge.com

Contents

Boobs 1
Don't Drive like a Twat this Springtime 3
The Twins 4
When First We Met 5
The Bishop of Bath and Wells 6
Balaclava 7
My Advice to Offenders 8
Ghosts 9
Goblins 10
The Monster in My Wardrobe 11
On Housework 12
When Granny Went to War 13
Never Date a Poet 15
My Cousin Martin 16
Billy's Pie 17
A Tale of Two Grannies 18
Ballet Boyz in the Theatre 20
Beyond Stupid Cupid 21
Shaving a Cat 22
Aunty Pat 23
Guildford 24
Katie's Drum Poem 26
The Brussels Sequence 27
Dallas Airport 28
Great Aunt Eve 29

Cardigan Bay	30
Fiddling	31
I Wish I Could Be Like the Poets of Now	32
When in Rome	33
In the Garden	34
Jollicles	35
Late Love	36
Vermont Limerick	37
Norman	38
Reminded of Mansfield	39
Spring in My Garden	40
Cake	42
A Pedant's Love Poem	43
I Sent You Chocolates	44
The Ballad of Cutlass and Big Red	45
The Human Condition	48

Boobs

My boobs have never been what you call big,
Unlike my friend Julie's; she paid for her rig.
They were massive and ripe, a triple F cup,
She looked like Mae West but she couldn't stand up.
She kept tipping over, with frightful abandon;
At least her big boobs gave her something to land on.
But she was persuasive; she told me I'd be
Much less of a woman, without surgery.

I went to the surgeon, the signs I misread -
"What's that bulge in your pants?", "It's my wallet," he said.
"I'll slice and I'll dice your pathetic wee boobs,
Then I'll drill and I'll fill them with old inner tubes,
Then I'll pump them with silicon formed into rounds,
Then I'll charge you the fee which is ten thousand pounds.
Nipples are extra, one lump or two?"
I made my excuses and cried in the loo.

I mused on the issue and, even if wealthy,
There's no way I'd fuck up my boobs, 'cos they're healthy.
They do the job well, they fill up a bra,
Blokes say that they're lovely; they're fine how they are.

So what if you lie down and witness your tits
Slop sideways and backwards down into your pits?
So what if they're weeny, a pair of fried eggs
Popped out by the teeniest hen on two legs?
You can be confident they won't explode
On economy seats on the way back from Rhodes.
You can be certain that each time you sneeze
Those silicon bastards won't shoot round your knees.

So, when you see boobs with a person attached,
And you know that your own ones are very
    mismatched,
Stick your hand down your bra for a bit of a feel.
Your tits might be weird but at least they are real.

Don't Drive like a Twat this Springtime

This is my protest poem. I am very moderate.

Don't drive like a twat this springtime,
Don't mow down a badger or two,
Don't squash a hesitant bunny,
Just to get first in the queue.

So what if you're late for your meeting
Or the last seat has gone on the train?
Some bunnies will still have their mummy,
So slow down on that nasty chicane.

It's been proven by rigorous science
That good drivers have lovely bums,
Kind drivers are terribly clever
And bad ones are terribly dumb.

All the squirrels, frogs, pigeons and foxes
And winged hairy thingies like that
Will sing your praises forever,
'Cos you didn't drive like a twat.

The Twins

My twin sisters don't like this poem. I don't know why. Our mum's not even called Belle.

When both the twins drowned in the lake
Their mama, Belle, swore she would die.
She would have rescued them, but her
French manicure was not yet dry.

When First We Met

This is an important poem, as it shows I am a proper poet. Firstly, it's about love and loss, and when you apply for your Poetic Licence, you have to demonstrate that 87% of your output is about love and loss. 13% should be about daffodils, evidently. Secondly, it's called "When First We Met." Normal people would write "When We First Met" but no, I am a poet and have to be needlessly difficult. Thirdly, it's written in iambic pentameter so it's practically Shakespeare.

When first we met, we knew we were in lust;
Our common interest in whips and chains,
Our joint delight in being bound and trussed,
Our savouring of every ounce of pain.
But now you're dead and everything is wrong.
I thought your screams were screams of ecstasy.
Turns out our safe word was a bit too long:
Cholangiopancreatography.

The Bishop of Bath and Wells

This is a religious poem. I hope I don't offend you. Oh, I don't care.

The Bishop of Bath and Wells was reclining
Upon my chaise longue in the parlour.
Naked, apart from his thong, he was dining
On imported whelk from Kampala.
He said to me, "John," (he was no good at names,)
"There's this holy tract by St Augustine
That says Belgians are evil," but, ere he could finish,
The Pope and four cardinals bust in.

"Oi Bish!" said a cardinal, Monsignor Jacques Marie Choufleur a.k.a Stan,
"We know what you're hiding under your tract -
A Madonna and Child by Cezanne."
However, although this story's exciting
I don't really know where it's going,
So I think I'd prefer to finish it here
And be happy with really not knowing.

Balaclava

This poem is avant-garde because it doesn't rhyme. This is also a true story, because, as a poet, I deal in truth.

I have three brothers.
When they were little, my Mum gave them short, sensible crew cut hair styles
And warm balaclavas for cold days.
With their balaclavas off, they looked like little thugs.
With their balaclavas on, they looked like little armed robbers.
But we didn't notice that then
Because those were the Good Old Days,
Because balaclavas were allowed.
These days, it's not socially acceptable to wear a balaclava.
But I wear one.
I wear mine indoors. I wear mine in the bath.
My bath toys assume I am an armed robber
And they are afraid.

My Advice to Offenders

I'm a poet at the other end of the scale from Carol Ann Duffy, i.e. not famous, and you will see why in a minute. Here's my unasked-for and misinformed opinion on the offenders' books debate of 2014 in the UK. It's in poorly rhymed poem format.

The great and the good have decided
That you don't get no books at all
'Cos all you'll do is pile 'em high
To try to climb over the wall.

So, to conceal your block and tackle in,
Swap your snout for a bloody big tome.
Something fat like *The Stud* by Jacqueline
Collins, sister of Joan.

Ghosts

To children, who are sore afraid
That night-time ghosts will get them:
Fear not, the monsters who will eat
Your brains at night won't let them.

Goblins

Ghosts and goblins, ghouls and trolls:
From these we can't protect you.
We're going to the Rose and Crown
We're going to get wrecked. You
Might just want to lock the door.
Me and your dad will be back about four.

The Monster in My Wardrobe

There are monsters in my wardrobe
When I draw my curtains.
The aliens with the anal probe
Are lurking there, I'm certain.
The zombies and the vampires too
Are waiting where I put my shoes.
But the things that make my poor blood freeze
Are my '80s stone-washed dungarees.

On Housework

I'm outraged because I'm a poet and shouldn't have to do housework.

I'm a stranger to housework.
It's just such a pain
To clean things. They'll only
Get dirty again.

I don't want to Hoover
When I'm working on my oeuvre.
Poet Boris Pasternak
Never did the Shake 'n' Vac.
Shakespeare didn't have to dust
And William Wordsworth didn't bust
A gut to wipe the window sills
When writing about daffodils.
I could write an Alex Pope
If I had slaves, like Wendy Cope.
If I didn't have to wash a plate
I could be Poet Laureate.

When Granny Went to War

Granny died a hero; she didn't die in vain.
She liberated Monaco and northern parts
   of Spain.
Her sponge pudding was to die for and lots of
   baddies did,
Overrun by custard, banana slices hid.

Machine gun nest was no match
For her batch
Of delicious fruit scones.
Served by reserves at an unaccustomed pace
On doilies, despoiling enemy faces.
They gave up. And ate up. And joined our side of the
   table.

A secret weapon: her own recipe.
The enemy tried Delia, Julia, Nigella and Mary,
But none so scary
As Granny's Death by Chocolate.

Sitting knitting at Balaclava;
Knit! purl! knit! purl! - her needles cast with
   lightning speed
A web of cable that bound and surrounded the
   enemy
And marched them east.

Quick, lads! Lavender hankies at ten o'clock!
Too late. Overcome by scents they senseless fall
Scooped up and shut up behind knitted walls
For the duration.

A crochet ricochet wounds her;
A stitch here and there and she's back to the front
Replying in kind to the howitzer.
A mortar of rock cakes, baked shock troops,
Blazing raisins razing the foe to the floury ground.

We lost her in that floury cloud.
Marching with circular needle curling around her
    shoulder,
She was never seen again.
We won the war but lost our gran.

And now we are how she was then
And we remember and are sad.
Her recipes, at least, live on,
Bite-sized reminders of the times
When oppressors got their just desserts.

Never Date a Poet

Never date a poet,
The evidence is strong.
Don't think about how nice they seem,
To date a poet is wrong.
Their pathological desire
To express love and pain
Means every private thing you do
Becomes public domain.

The first time that they kiss you
They'll write a loving sonnet
About your second favourite bra
With the ketchup stains upon it.
They'll write that you smell sweeter than
The perfumes of Arabia,
Then compose a limerick
In homage to your labia.

And when, of course, you tire of them,
Make sure that they dump you
Or risk a rash of vengeful poems
Of things that just aren't true.

Like stories of you fondling nuns
Or shaving little kittens
Or topping pups with melted cheese,
Gluing babies to their mittens,
Or taking from the petty cash
To fuel your old crack habit
Or caught out by the RSPCA
In flagrante with your rabbit.

Your friends will all disown you;
They won't know that it's a fit up.
So never date a poet
Or kill them when you split up.

My Cousin Martin

When my cousin Martin was buried alive
And cried "Let me out!" to his great uncle Clive,
He might as well have been shouting to air.
Clive's hearing appliance had gone for repair.

Billy's Pie

Billy's sister stole his pie
And choked with sweat upon her brow.
But when he saw the chewed-up crust
Said Billy, "I don't want it now."

A Tale of Two Grannies

This is a tale of two grannies.
Flo is old fashioned, clay owl in each cranny.
June is more avant-garde, raving with trannies.
Which one should look after my kids?

Traditional Flo finds the Daily Mail calming.
Her casual racism's rather alarming:
"Mr Patel at the shop is quite charming.
The others can get the boat home."

But her cherry Pavlova and scones are delicious,
Her stews, soups and salads extremely nutritious,
Her attention to appetite borders on vicious.
My kids would be very well fed.

But her horrid faux-pas with my gay friends
 are legion,
Thinks Skype's a disease of the genital region,
Blames pot-pourri on "those awful Norwegians,"
I can't give my darlings to her.

My other gran, June, is a modern romantic,
Poetic, frenetic, likes sex which is Tantric.
Her passion for Bono is bloody gigantic.
She curses much more than I do.

But she's confidence-boosting and bursting with
 vigour,
Her discussions are argued with fairness and rigour,
She cuts an unbiased and positive figure.
My kids will think well of themselves.

But she's pierced in ten places, hair bleached like a
 bimbo,
Runs womanhood workshops, vaginas akimbo.
She gave me a glittery dildo for Chrimbo.

I can't have my kids go to her.

I ponder the problem, alone in the chippy.
I don't want my kids to be Nazis or hippies.
I've got the answer, why am I so dippy?
Look after the buggers myself.

Ballet Boyz in the Theatre

This poem was inspired by going to see the Ballet Boyz, who are men who dance. I like dance and I like men so I had a nice evening. I also like dinosaurs but I don't think that show exists, yet.

Ballet Boyz in the theatre
Bare chests
And lean, muscular arms
And wiry dancer physiques.
In your flesh-coloured tights
It looks like you are dancing naked.
That's worth the price of a front row seat.

It's so nice to see men dancing *together*.
They dance vulnerability and grace
And all the things women are allowed to be, all the time.
They dance power, strength and teamwork
And all the things women might like to be shown doing more of.
To be honest, I've got to fix that sentence.

My gaze is 40% amazement, 30%   appreciation and 30% ogling.
I rather like the Italian one.
I will stare at him.
And stare. And stare.
Oh, he's noticed. I've unnerved him. He's fallen.
I should probably take my balaclava *off*.

I didn't see the end of the show as I was shown out during the interval.

Beyond Stupid Cupid

Cupid's not stupid but downright retarded.
I wasn't protected, my bum was unguarded.
He fired his big arrow but missed and his dart
Went into my buttcheek not into in my heart.
That's why my affairs are such bloody failures.
Men hide to avoid me or move to Australia.
But you, you are different, you're not like the others
Who are looking for trophies or girls like their
    mothers.
You lovingly watch me, your gaze holding mine,
Your gentleness calming, your silence sublime.
You put up with my rantings and endless
    complaining.
Not needy, not proud, you don't care if it's raining.
We've never had problems or troubles or teething;
Sometimes I wish you were alive and still breathing.

Shaving a Cat

My friends Elizabeth and Patrick needed an emergency New Year poem for a neighbour. This was the best I could do. I think their neighbour is still speaking to them.

Every New Year is a time for reflection,
For thinking of new friends and old.
As neighbours, you're held in our highest affection;
We think it is time you were told.

Last August, when you went on summer vacation
And left us in charge with the keys,
We kind of gave in to all sorts of temptation
And it wasn't just pinching some cheese.

Every day and some nights we let ourselves in.
Our motto was clear; "Let the party begin!"
We drank your best Beaujolais, left your Blue Nun,
We bust your blue Spode with our submachine gun.
Patrick tried on your knickers and wore your stilettos
While I smoked some weed with my friends from the ghettoes.
I bathed in your perfume and used your toothbrush.
We all used your toilet and never once flushed.
We shagged on your bed, we're not proud of that,
But it was only by accident that we shaved the cat.

So our New Year wish is to ask for your pardon
And hope you don't know what we did in your garden.

Aunty Pat

This is a true story.

Aunty Pat had a rat skin hat
Together with a rat skin glove.
But nastily she died, ripped apart from the inside
By a rat with a Kalashnikov.

Guildford

With apologies to Rupert Brooke and everyone who lives not in Guildford.

God, I will pack and skip so free,
To get the number 63
To travel up the 281
To Guildford, where my heart belongs.
For Guildford is so fair of face
Inhabited by a gifted race
Of mummies in their four by fours,
A polished knocker on each door.
And Guildford people are so clean
And live their gentle lives serene.

For Dorking people rarely wash
And folk in Chilworth? Just not posh.
In Aldershot they download porn;
Their kids will pee upon your lawn.
And Bramley men, who dine on stoat,
Will steal your purse and shag your goat.
And those in Shalford, even worse,
Will steal your goat and shag your purse.
And Ripley women, after dark,
Leave their knickers in Stoke Park.
The nightly practices in Send
Would drive a psycho round the bend.
Strong men scream and fall to bits
When girls from Woking flash their tits.
And weekend Romeos, puking beer,
Are from Ash Vale, and not from here.

But Guildford folk, with calm reserve
Delight in chess and quince preserve
Are always proper and refined
To nannies, au pairs and their kind.
For cultured they, and quiet of manner;
No tattoos, piercings or bandanas.

A bunch of intellectual farts
With poems at the Bar des Arts.
The High Street clock stands ten to three
and are there cupcakes, still, for tea?

Katie's Drum Poem

My drumming friend Katie Stephenson uses a poem to help children learn about rhythm. We mucked about with it and came up with this:

Juice
Biscuit
Toblerone
Double Decker
Chocolate Éclair
Hyperglycaemia

The Brussels Sequence

My copywriting friends, Paul Holder and Lara Groves, and I were bored one Christmas lunchtime, and came up with an important contribution to haiku culture. Lara hates Brussels sprouts. Can you guess which is the verse she wrote?

Come, friends, and let us
Praise the sprout in all its forms.
Boiled. That's it, really.

What about breakfast?
Little balls quick fried with spuds:
Bubble and sprout squeak.

Girdle the little
Green with fine shortcrust pastry;
Lo! Sprout Wellington.

Put the kettle on
Dried balls, water to the line,
Pot Sprout for students.

Sin, scraped from the tongue,
Bitterness inspires puke.
Sprout, you win again.

Who would have thought a
Tiny cabbage engenders
Such discordant views?

Dallas Airport

My friend Elizabeth Molineux texted me from Dallas Airport. She had been visiting her family and had eaten a lot of pie, as you do when you are there. She felt too full to complete her journey home. This is my response:

Here I sit in Dallas airport.
I am much too fat to fly.
"Why is that? " I bet you all thought.
I had too much fucking pie.

(P.S. If you say "Jeetcha Pah?" it sounds like "Did you eat your pie?" in Texan.)

Great Aunt Eve

This is very rude.

It's always a pleasure to see Great Aunt Eve.
She's kind and she's wrinkly but very naive.
She keeps saying rude things but doesn't mean to
So we stifle a giggle or pop to the loo.

At tea time she told us about her old muff.
"It's beaver," she said, "and it's getting quite rough.
I can still get both hands in, and so can your dad
'Cos he helped me to clean it with an old Brillo pad.
But it's getting rancid and starting to smell;
I should Cillit Bang it and bleach it as well."

Changing the subject (my smirking was plain)
Asked, "How was your birthday with Great Uncle Wayne?"
"Oh, so nice," she said, "His spending was reckless
Gave me a huge ring and a lovely pearl necklace.
He really splashed out on me, gave me a toast
With champagne when his friends and I had a spit roast."

She saw we were giggling; our faces were red,
So we told her the meanings of all that she'd said.
She gasped, "Girls, you're dreadful, thinking those words
Are dirty and nasty. How daft and absurd!
But I really must go now, it's past five and Wayne'll
Be worrying soon, 'cos I promised him anal."

Cardigan Bay

When I was much younger, the men I impressed
And I was artistic; I did it in style.
The vicar, especially, liked me to undress
One layer off at a time, to beguile.
My cardigan off in Cardigan Bay,
My petticoat off in Petticoat Lane,
My vest in the vestry, my pants in the pantry
But I wrapped up warm in the depths of the country.

Fiddling

This is a very learned poem as it is in Petrarchian sonnet form.

In truth, my friend, I love you, more or less.
More than a bowl of giblets served with Spam,
Much less than carrot cake or bramble jam.
Perhaps the same as my third favourite dress.

I cannot truly say where passion goes.
Perhaps your love of Arsenal's gone too far.
Perhaps you pass me by to kiss your car,
While I ignore your chat and paint my toes.

While this relationship is gathering dust
The best-before date long gone ten times over,
The clock is ticking our lives down to zero.
We could be free to choose a life of lust
For living, laughing, loving deep in clover,
But we just fiddle while life burns, like Nero.

I Wish I Could Be Like the Poets of Now

This is a lament, so if you laugh you're not intellectual.
Reading this aloud is like chewing a big chunk of Thornton's
toffee when you are wearing somebody else's teeth.

I wish I could be like the poets of now,
Who roll billowing, mellowing words from the tips
Of their tongues and the depths of their hearts.
Whose internal rhyming and driving of language
    flows forwards,
When all I want is to rhyme hearts with farts.

I wish I could be like the poets of now,
With filigree consonants, exquisite choices of voices
    reflecting,
Refracting, redacting emotions and notions
    expressed through their vowels.
Gestures conducting invisible orchestras,
Delivery urging and beckoning, ending lines in that
    unfinished way….
And all I can think is that vowels rhymes with
    bowels.

I wish I could be like the poets of now,
Whose feelings and dealings with life are organically
Melded with language or stoic, heroically hunt
Through vocabulary, seeking that nuance,
When all I can think is that hunt rhymes
With that word that's now in our heads but we can't
    say out loud.

I wish I could be like the poets of now,
With mysterious, serious metaphors echoing,
Glancing and dancing down artistic corridors
Ever away from me; those doors are shut to me.
My poesy only sophisticated smuttery.
I wish I could be like the poets of now.

When in Rome

When in Rome
Write a poem.

In the Garden

This was my first ever poem for no reason. Praise be!

In the garden, in the garden
Lay a naked Javier Bardem
And sultry on my climbing rose
Was Jonny Depp, without his clothes
And rampant in my lettuce patch
An undressed Sherlock, Cumberbatch
And quite delightful, perched upon
My shed, a bare Hollander, Tom.

You must agree it would be awesome
To fool around with this nice foursome
But what delights lay in the freesia
I could not tell, with my amnesia.
If I had not mislaid my specs
I would be having all the sex.
I would have spied them in their glory
And could have told a different story.
But time and age have proved a pain
And losing things becomes a bane
When socks are in the pot for tea
And keys are where they shouldn't be.

My neighbour told me of the pack
Of naked actors round the back
And when I ran there, agitated,
Found that none of them had waited.
So now, forlornly, by the Aga,
I tell my friends of that sad saga,
That sunny day, when, in the garden,
There lay a naked Javier Bardem.

Jollicles

When I went for a scan of my lady areas, the nice radiologist got very excited for me that I had two follicles left. I thought 'follicles' was such a jolly, happy word. When I got home I looked at Wikipedia to find out what follicles were. Then I wrote this poem, called "Jollicles." Can you see what I did there?

Two follicles left! Two follicles left!
How jolly, two follicles, how categorically
Weird and freaky and slightly unnerving
That I am still ripe for the pleasures of birthing.

Never considered my latent fertility,
Forgot to have kids; could never be bothered.
The spectre of spreading my genes never hovered
Across my to-do list; my body clock pleading
For toast and tequila but not for breast feeding.

Two follicles left; what names shall I give them?
Gomorrah and Sodom are far too Old Testament.
Perhaps something feminine, just like a fairy,
Like Daisy? No, too *Little House on the Prairie*.

Two follicles left! I know they're not babies;
I'm quite glad of that 'cos I'd rather have rabies.
It's just weird that I have them; it makes me
    feel girly.
But so does a Flake and a nice Curly Wurly.

Late Love

You get ten points for spotting the words that sound really good in a Geordie accent. My mum's a Geordie so it might slip through; it's genetic.

You took me off the shelf,
Gave me a damn good dusting,
But age has crept up further still,
Now our equipment's rusting.

With arthritis, bursitis and conjunctivitis,
It's terribly hard to be sexy or rude.
It takes me an hour to get in position.
I forget why I'm there, which ruins the mood.

We'll just have to face it, our sex life is passed.
The spirit is willing, the flesh can't be arsed.
Let's have a McVitie's Digestive and see
If Midsomer Murders is back on TV.

(The words that sound excellent in Geordie are arthritis, bursitis and conjunctivitis. You might also like to consider Guatemala and Kodacolour Gold.)

Vermont Limerick

There was a young man of Vermont,
Whose limericks never would rhyme.
When they asked why this was,
He replied, "I don't know,
I can't do last lines either."

Norman

This is world's silliest poem.

Norman Borman, the doormen foreman,
   married
Alma Palmer, the llama calmer,
   whose dad was
Farmer Palmer, the pyjama charmer,
   who married
Tina Mina, the wiener cleaner,
   who was stepmum to
Leif McGeef, the beef thief,
   who was friends with
Mark Stark, the park clerk,
   who was in love with
Sheila Wheeler, the peeler stealer,
   who shared a flat with
Una Tuna, the schooner crooner,
   who was going out with
Macca Knacker, the cracker packer,
   but fancied
Norman Borman, the doormen foreman,
   who campaigned for the rights of
Glenda Bender, the fender tender,
   whose boss was
Cilla Miller, the gorilla killer,
   who was jealous of
Una Tuna, the schooner crooner,
   and shot
Norman Borman, the doormen foreman,
   and made everybody sad.

Reminded of Mansfield

It's about the weather. Oh, and there's a literary echo; see if you can get it. It's very intellectual.

March. Cold. Wet. Crap.
Dirty British weather with a rain-soaked outlook,
Cutting through my onesie in a damp-draught haze.
With a legacy of chilblains,
    mildew, Chapstick,
Moist socks, silverfish and train delays.
March. Cold. Wet. Crap.

Spring in My Garden

It's not a garden.
It's the place where plants go to die.
It's the space where failure and inconsistency meet.
It's where optimism commits annual suicide.
It's the final resting place of hope.
People say you have to be born with green fingers;
I say if you are born with green fingers you have
   circulation issues.

My garden in spring - the antidote to Giverny.
Monet said, "My garden is my masterpiece."
Monet can go fuck himself.
Next door can go fuck herself, too.
She is out there every day
Trimming her bush,
Wielding her secateurs like the French-sounding
   things that they are.
Her lawns are smooth and green,
Her Albertines, the Sherpas of the climbing
   rose world.
Her and her garden-centre Versailles.
My only comfort is that she is old.
Everyone knows old people are good at gardening
Because old people know when it's time to get used
   to the cold, welcoming earth.

My garden in spring.
It's a mockery
Of a rockery.
I plant sweet basil, I get stinking mugwort.
Or mugwurt. I don't know how to say it.
No one does.
My garden is no Eden.
No birds of paradise strut
Around my water butt,
Home to things as yet unnamed by science.
My rambling rose has rambled out,

And the only creeper in my garden is Colin the
 Pervert from Number 17.
He would have peed on my dahlias, had they lived.

My garden in spring.
No right-thinking sparrow makes an appearance,
No mentally sound blackbird trills and tweets from
 sunlit forsythia.
There are no tits round my nuts
And nothing has touched my fat balls.

So, sling the dead badger in the compost, my love,
While I delouse the slugs,
For it is spring in my garden.

Cake

This is another true story.

My mate Maria wandered in
And sampled my banana bread.
She licked her lips and with a grin
Said "Moist." "It's only cake," I said.

A Pedant's Love Poem

Roses are red
But also come in many other colours.
Violets tend to be blue
But you can also get yellow, white and cream;
While some types are bi-coloured.
Sugar is sweet
To humans whose G-protein-coupled taste receptors
    are functioning well.
And you wouldn't taste sweet.
In fact, you would probably taste like pork, which
    isn't particularly sweet
Unless you load it with apple sauce.
But I still love you.

I Sent You Chocolates

I sent you chocolates; you fed them to your geese.
You threw away the flowers I sent, so pretty.
I sent you diamonds, yet you called in the police;
Could be because I sent you that dead kitty.

The Ballad of Cutlass and Big Red

As there is no sex or swearing in this poem but a lot of violence, I am assuming this is a poem for children. I am sorry about that. It's quite long so if you need a wee, cork it. Also, technically, it's not a ballad but I wrote it before I knew what ballad form was.

I sing of ferrets and a man
Whose favourite dish was bunny flan.
Daily, daily was his habit
To eat a meal containing rabbit.
Daily, daily without fail
Consumed all bits but bunnies' tail
Which he strung up with bunny wool,
To contemplate when feeling full.

This bloke was called the Ferret Man
And with good reason, for his plan
Was to destroy all bunny-kind
With ferrets, so, with this in mind,
He'd send his ferrets underground
To maul and kill the buns they found
And all the buns they couldn't get
Were chased into the waiting net.

But bunnies are flufflesome, fuzzy and sweet
So pleasant to cuddle, too lovely to eat.
With gleamy bright eyes and twitchery noses
Bunnies shed niceness wherever they goeses.
The sort of small bunnies that make you
    go squeeeeeeeeeeeeeeeee
The Ferret Man wants in a pie for his tea.
But today's bunnies were different; genetically
    strange,
They'd interbred lots with a really weird range
Of dangerous animals: dragons and geese
And crocodiles, tigers and bees from Dumfries.

Ferret Man was ready.
His nets were moored.
The rhythm different
To stop you getting bored.

Ferret One was called Cutlass, because of his teeth.
They were sharp and were nasty, no pity beneath.
He'd catch hold of a bunny and slice through her neck
And drink all her blood. How unseemly, by heck!

While Cutlass was underground, Ferret Man burned
For the meal he would have when Cutlass returned.
Yes, Bunny Wellington, Bunny en Croute,
Bunny Lasagne, or bunny and fruit.
Chilli con Bunny and Moules Bunnulaire,
Bunny in a Basket and Bunny Éclair.

He waited a minute then waited for ten,
Then another ten minutes, a minute again.
The Ferret Man shuffled and gave a sharp shout:
"Cutlass come back!" but no Cutlass came out.

Ferret Man scowled and brought out a sack,
A reinforced one with chain mail round the back.
Carefully, gingerly, avoiding an injury,
He pulled out the noisomemost, fearsomemost ferret of all:
A scarily, hairily ferret with claws
That would rip you to pieces, and Rottweiler jaws
That'd cling to your buttocks and never let go;
And on top of all that, a bad case of BO.
Big Red was his name, he was vicious and nasty.
(He bit off my finger which he ate in a pasty!)

Big Red bared his teeth and, with a great roar,
Scorched down the warren, as Cutlass before.
Ferret Man waited a minute then ten, then another
Ten minutes, a minute again.

The Ferret Man shuffled and gave a sharp shout:
"Big Red, come back!" but no Big Red came out.

The Ferret Man waited the rest of the day;
Got hungry, got cross and then went on his way.
Ferretless, listless, he made it back home
And had nothing to eat but the bunny tailbones.

The Ferret Man choked on the dry bunny tails.
His lips went bright blue, his skin deathly pale
And no one was near to hear of his cries.
He was found four weeks later, covered in flies.
And at the same time that the Ferret Man died
The bunnies were eating the ferrets, deep fried.
So Cutlass and Big Red and Ferret Man, too,
All ended badly, so let us review:
The moral of this story is: don't be a meanie,
Don't mess with a bun; you'll end up a panini.

The Human Condition

This poem is called 'The Human Condition'. This is a very important poem as it reflects our shared struggles and triumphs as human beings. If you want to do this poem properly, you read out the first three lines of each verse, and your friends shout out the "I've done that!" bit.

I got up late this morning
I broke my jaw with yawning
I farted without warning
I've done that.

Shot ferrets out of season
Got married without reason
Did twenty years for treason
I've done that.

I've started doing jogging
I've spent my summers logging
I've tried a bit of dogging
I've done that.

I've frolicked with Francesco
I've skinny-dipped al fresco
Nicked tellies out of Tesco
I've done that.

I broke my hip at Twister
I bought a frog in Bicester
I murdered my twin sister
I've done that.

I fell off Brighton pier
I've been trapped in Ikea
Caught rampant gonorrhea
I've done that.

I've tangoed 'til I'm giddy
I've partied with P Diddy
I've fiddled with a kiddy
I've done that.

P.S. This poem isn't really called 'The Human Condition'; it's called 'The Kiddy Fiddler Call and Return'. But I didn't want to write that down anywhere in case Google was watching.

THE END

Surprise!

Lorna

There was a young lady called Lorna
Who stripped off her top in the sauna.
To a round of applause
She whipped off her drawers
And pulled out some flora and fauna.

More stuff from Louise Etheridge

Paperbacks available from Amazon and Waterstones:

More Slightly Wrong
Happy Stories for Busy People

For Kindle and other e-readers and most computers, available from Amazon:

Slightly Wrong
More Slightly Wrong
Happy Stories for Busy People

Louise's poemtastic website:
www.louiseetheridge.com

Facebook: **www.facebook.com/LouiseDoesWords**
Twitter @**LouEtheridge**

Louise is a lyricist and sings with The Dirty Carols.
www.thedirtycarols.co.uk

www.ingramcontent.com/pod-product-compliance
Lightning Source LLC
Chambersburg PA
CBHW031503040426
42444CB00007B/1192